To Terrie
For all we share,
now + always!
love,
Barb

To Terrie,

for the love of

poetry!

# The Only Gift to Bring

Poems by John Fox

Seasonings Press

**Acknowledgements:**
"When Someone Deeply Listens to You" previously appeared in *Finding What You Didn't Lose: Expressing Your Truth and Creativity Through Poem-Making*. (Inner Work Books, 1995)

**Invitation:**
If you would like to support The Institute for Poetic Medicine, and its mission to awaken soulfulness in the human voice, send your 501c3 tax-deductible donation to The Institute for Poetic Medicine, P.O. Box 60189, Palo Alto, CA 94306.

Cover and page design: Valerie Knight Design
Photo credit: John Skillen

ISBN: 978-163443863-6

For information about permission to reproduce selections from this book, write to John Fox at jfoxcpt@aol.com or P.O. Box 60189, Palo Alto, CA 94306.

The Only Gift to Bring   Copyright ©2015 by John Fox, CPT
All rights reserved.
Printed in the United States of America.

*This book is dedicated to Jeremy Tarcher.*

## Appreciations

My thanks to Michael S. Glaser for his beautiful support, wise editorial discernment and fine sense of composition.

What leads me forward are thousands of people who I have had the blessing and good fortune to work with over a thirty-four year career of poetry and healing. I am grateful for each person's willingness to write, express vulnerability & strength and share the reclamation of their truest voice. Humility and inspiration join here and that joining helps me on my journey of soul-making. Here is where I learn and find motivation to do my part to build the beloved community.

To friends, people unknown to me as our paths cross, colleagues with whom I have had the privilege to work, anyone who inspires these poems, who has challenged me to grow through them, thank you.

Thanks to Valerie Knight for her fine design of this book.

I especially would like to express appreciation to Holly Fox, my late eldest sister, for her joy, humor and deep nature.

## A Note About These Poems

These poems are selections of my writing from 1974 to the present. For many reasons a chronological approach to their arrangement was awkward, so Michael composed them as one might movements of musical score. As it turns out, the first poem in the chapbook is also my earliest. The last poem, *Poetry* (written in 1999), is inspired by my reflection on the first poem I wrote at the age of thirteen. I was watching a girl skate at Thornton Park in Shaker Heights, Ohio. Such time-shifting and juxtaposition feels creative, whole and true-to-life. There is something about the deeply layered and permeable nature of poetic language that makes a poem uniquely capable of breathing free of the constrictions and linear limitations of time and space.

That skater, gliding into a leap with a focused determination and courage, to give *everything* to gravity and grace, represents for me what making poems is all about as I meet and relate with this nearly indescribable life. This small selection of my work gathers together my life-journey. I would like to share this journey with you, where poetry acts in a sacred and healing way: as medicine, companion and place.

– John Fox

I look for the way
things will turn
out spiraling from a center,
the shape
things will take to come forth in…

> A. R. Ammons
> from *Poetics*

# Contents

Nurse! Nurse! Nurse! .................................................................. 1
Climbing the Yei Bei Cheii Trail ................................................ 2
A Poem Waits at Its Own Core .................................................. 3
Driving to Bethlehem ................................................................ 4
When Someone Deeply Listens To You .................................... 5
Everything Is a Surprise ............................................................. 6
Holly's Life & Death Were Made of Panache ........................... 7
Days of Rain ............................................................................... 8
When Jewels Sing ....................................................................... 9
Inez Corbin ............................................................................... 10
Consider What Happens .......................................................... 11
The Only Gift To Bring ............................................................ 12
The Marrow of Who I Am ....................................................... 13
What Understanding Won't Help ........................................... 14
Sycamore Leaves ...................................................................... 15
Faith ........................................................................................... 16
My Mother's Last Days ............................................................ 17
Cardinal .................................................................................... 18
In the Deep Days of Fall .......................................................... 19
The Holiness of Wood ............................................................. 20
There Is an Origin (and) Home Equity ................................... 21
Prayer for a Quiet Mind and an Open Heart ......................... 22
For a Friend Whose Faith in Me Is Like. . . ............................ 23
Blown Home ............................................................................ 24
Lift Up the Banner ................................................................... 25
Poetry ........................................................................................ 26

## Nurse! Nurse! Nurse!
    (Night Shift)
                *to Judy*

She moves quickly toward the little boy
turtled on his back in a hip-length cast.
Her dark blue-sweatered arms
attending to the moment,
reach to touch and turn him with a soft voice.
She makes him more comfortable,
more a part of herself, so late into the night.

## Climbing the Yei Bei Cheii Trail, The Path of the Holy Ones at Canyon de Chelly

*for Jon and Lupita McClanahan*

One foot in front of the other.
This foothold and then the next
Or whatever will do in the moment—

And in these, my wobbly steps,
Some very old embarrassment
Shudders to the surface

Of my heart pumping hard
But nowhere as deep
As the place in me

That is
Whole,
That is
Already home.

## A Poem Waits at Its Own Core

The poem at its core
Is snow or egg,
The new moon or grass
In spring.

All these pause at the edge
Of change. There is a deep
Stillness you must pass through
To get close to what waits.

At this edge, you leave
Everything behind
Except what the poem needs:
Warmth, rain, silence,
Gravity.

Make it something you know
Only for the first time:
A river, heartbeat,
Cradle, field of play—
The place where all things
Begin again.

## Driving to Bethlehem
*to Naomi Shihab Nye*

I will not forget driving by
two small children,
little boys perched
on top of a donkey,
riding all by themselves
along the side
of a loosely graveled road,
desolate and barren,
between Jerusalem
and Bethlehem.

I realized, at that moment,
zooming to Bethlehem,
how much of the Holy Land
I was missing.

## When Someone Deeply Listens to You

When someone deeply listens to you
it is like holding out a dented cup
you've had since childhood
and watching it fill up with
cold, fresh water.
When it balances on top of the brim,
you are understood.
When it overflows and touches your skin,
you are loved.

When someone deeply listens to you
the room where you stay
starts a new life
and the place where you wrote
your first poem
begins to glow in your mind's eye.
It is as if gold has been discovered!

When someone deeply listens to you
your bare feet are on the earth
and a beloved land that seemed distant
is now at home within you.

## Everything Is a Surprise
*for Shelley, my sister*

Death might be a moment
where being *everything* you are
is met by a welcome Surprise
and by a discovery you make
that it was, or actually
is perfectly fine
to be who you are,
is more than all right,
and it is only this Surprise
and your discovery of it
that went missing for awhile
in your life, or was so long
but not entirely forgotten.
But when Surprise meets you,
you discover that Everything
opens its arms wide to you,
pauses for a moment, even
steps back slightly to await
your arrival, gives you a moment to see,
and yes you will run forward,
full tilt, aware you might as well
keep running hard like that
because what else is there to do now,
aware, and even more, feeling assured
you could never knock Everything over
and are, at the same moment,
about to discover Everything
will never let you fall.

## Holly's Life & Death Were Made of Panache

(In the final moment of Edmond Rostand's play *Cyrano de Bergerac*, Cyrano, declares he has one thing left without spot or wrinkle that he can call his own…)

*Et, c'est…mon panache*
Cyrano de Bergerac

*What now?!*
Holly Fox

Your last action
in this life
was to fling
your breath out
the very last one
singular and
specific, a whole
lifetime felt
in what you flung
forward, this invisible
inspiration
skipped hard
& struck the moment's
surface, then gone
and done, to disappear
into depthlessness.

And immediately
I thought of the way
you kicked
your sneakers off
with a deliberate
panache, that was
uniquely your own
in a gesture of delight,
confident
in your powers
to give flight, a carefree
challenge to gravity's
grave utility,
making sure your day
came to a close
with joy unfettered.

## Days of Rain

> *Open me up to feel due words*
> Phillip Booth

I want the losing it all
as when it rains hard.
I want letting it all loose;
to open myself
to the only true opener
of my freer falling feeling.

I want that dense drape of
drenched space to drop
into the entire air,
the atmosphere, the ache, fall
there, drawn, down, drowned
into the lowest ground

of the great and good grieving,
soaked into that low place
of kind green grass
and further then,
into the darker grit that gathers it,
the one who finally gets it:

who becomes exactly what it is,
the one who lets the grieving sound out
again, yet now, wholly held, returns it
to this singular heart-of-mine
that might, may, must
grow greater through love's loss.

## When Jewels Sing

Radiance results from earth's pressure:
with each moment's precision,
life works us into clear-cut uniqueness.

A community of precious human beings
with origins primitive and wild as diamonds,
faceted by skilled and invisible hands that turn us
upon a wheel dusted with God's bright dark silence,
we become men and women joined to walk
swarthy, holy, original and transparent.

Catching first light of day upon ourselves,
our voices sing of truth and loveliness
in response to vows first sung by stars.

## Inez Corbin

Every Friday Inez Corbin mopped mom's kitchen floor.
Her life was all about her face,
that dark delta of sorrow,
that moved slowly toward death,
yet with mellow radiance
a richness that filtered out poison and gave life.

Her presence was like the clean regal garment
set out for Jesus on Thursday evening.
Her face was full of love.

I could hear in her voice
a direction back to myself,
and I could hear in her voice
that nothing else mattered to her but love.

How she made her way in the world
in the harsh winter and hot summer
on those heavy legs given over to life
in folds over her knee high stockings,
given over to love, unbeautiful with love.

What she did for those she loved —
not lean cleverness, or sophistication —
it was a real love, dark love
that included me, brought me along,
saw I was more, that love
could be seen in my face too
and that any distance between us
in fact was not.

## Consider What Happens

Consider what happens
upon hearing a poem
that moves you. The nod
of your head, tucking
your chin close
to your chest, as if
stopping to rest, as if you could cry now
in the middle of a long journey.
Here, whatever you regret having forgotten
even with your aching tiredness
(which you cannot forget) all of a sudden
turns to a surprisingly vibrant sky
as your eyes widen ever-so-slightly
in a recognition that shimmers
under your skin, wells-up
into a calm line-of-sight
that is your own and goes on
almost forever.
Astonished, you walk outside breathing
and slowly stroll in the fresh air
suddenly aware that back in your house
someone new, a stranger you like,
has arrived.

## The Only Gift to Bring

Words are what you struggle past
in the nighttime
walking towards home,
where Silence lives
in lamplight
to greet you.

Listen.

Now there are no more words
to struggle through.
You don't have to think
of what words to lay out
to wear tomorrow.
Silence has never worn anything,

Listen.

Silence needs only
your being here.
Arms embrace inside
this atmosphere.

## The Marrow of Who I Am
for the mothers of soldiers killed in Lebanon, October 1983

*Forgiveness is holiness, by forgiveness the universe is held together.*
                                        Mahabharata

i

I hear the unbearable sorrow of mothers
abruptly leave this world,
escape into whatever sky is above the door
they open to solemn military men,
who bring bad news like an ancient Greek chorus.
Tears of anguish spill onto sofas
that do not matter anymore.
Grief rips the heart from every home's
special dream, as each mother suddenly wakens
into that terrible moment when masks are removed.

ii

The marrow of who I am
is a tree struck by the lightning
of anger and sadness, shattering
heartwood upon the earth.

The marrow of who I am
is made by the Mother
who stands at each and every door,
listening to love's undying cry
sink into her very heart.

The marrow of who I am
is always creating new blood,
a life innocent to this world,
safe in the mystery of forgiveness's home.

## What Understanding Won't Help

Does the dusk light
that rests for moments
upon the leaves of
a Japanese Maple
awaken your heart,
like it does mine?

And by "awaken"
I mean as if
loneliness were at least
willing to not give in
to despair, because
loss felt like a sure thing.

Could you stand there
at that edge with me
aware of & holding
these small realities of our day,
like a treasure
that will not last or give
us everything we want

but still deserves attention,
like the leaf that catches last light
and is lifted up to our sight
by a shadow
that silently cares for it,
and everything underneath
that can't be said?

## Sycamore Leaves

(November 1974, six months after the amputation of my right leg)

*The poetry of earth is never dead.*
John Keats

At eighteen, in my sense
of shame and grief,
I felt troubled and beyond repair.

The great stars, cold
and silent, were
as sleepless as I and as mute.

And stars were my only companions
on this strange earth, when
right before dawn

I walked through
an empty park in Brookline, Mass.
and some mercy called day

came for them
to come in from the cold.
Came for those stars

those silent and distant friends,
came for them,
not me.

I walked this ground
alone, all the way
to the park's edge

until I had nowhere else
to go, and then, why
I cannot explain:

I stopped. I bent down low,
(because with my artificial leg
it was not possible

to kneel) and I
picked up two wet
Sycamore leaves.

I picked them up
where they pressed their faces
upon the dark earth

and then pressed them
with my fingers
into my right palm,

and said a prayer asking
for their power to stir me
and stay with me

from that moment
until this one, stay forever,
in my deep memory.

Now, as if it were yesterday,
I feel the wet grit
of fallen Sycamore leaves

in my palm and I
stand here and there
with an urge to live.

*I think continually of those who were truly great...*
                                        Stephen Spender

## Faith

I think continually of those who step forward
in spite of chasms too close for comfort
their feet keep vigil upon
the humble earth and all its tears,
the dark tangled roots of
being alive, feet pushed down as if listening
to the presence of what finally matters:
fragile moments giving way like sand,
kind voices green as grass
and the deep strata of ageless strength
unseen. They move one step at a time,
even when their hearts, high up
in the spinning world are pounding, empty
of courage—walking along the edge,
where something is felt underneath: the faith
the unknown alone can give, these,
the footprints I follow.

## My Mother's Last Days

I am lying on my sleeping bag
under the stars at Canyon de Chelly
and thinking about my
mother, her last days,
her dying.

When things occurred, and when they didn't,
I noticed the way she lifted
her shoulders, paused ever-so-slightly,
smiled, and then, let her shoulders go.
One afternoon she added, "I feel completely at ease."

The feeling on her face,
and the language of her body,
was all about letting go.
Her smile held a rare edgelessness.

Her gesture, I believe was the sign of grace,
a lasting grace that chose to show itself to me
or perhaps a calm awareness transcending words,
that said even what mattered so much
wasn't going to anymore.

## Cardinal

"When John grows up, he's going to be a poet."
>my mother speaking to a group of people
>when I was in 8th grade

>>"I *am* a poet."
>>me, looking at her

The black of my eyes
and throat is a nighttime
that stretches into mystery.

>A deep unknowing
>of life beyond words.

>>I feel my way
>>into a flight path of silence
>>I am at home with

>>>where red wings fold in,
>>>to honor dusk, and extend to
>>>herald dawn.

>>>>This voice I have, this sure,
>>>>sweet and unmistakable
>>>>brightness of song.

## In the Deep Days of Fall

In the deep days of fall
I sometimes imagine Time
wakes up in the middle
of the night, sits on the edge
of a single bed, in faded pajamas,
leans down to pull on cracked high-top
leather shoes, laces untied, and tromps
down to the chilly kitchen with its
worn linoleum floor, and then down
basement stairs, damp and creaky,
walks over to the weathered cupboard
under the grimy ground level
window in the empty storeroom
and lifts the wrought iron latch
from the last century, opens
the cupboard and surveys
the quiet heap of seeds kept
for the future, held within
an assortment of containers:
an elegant tea cup from China,
a plain clay bowl made by his daughter,
a shimmering abalone shell
as a deep kindness comes over him
he leans his lined face close
to consider each carefully.
He sees light green colors,
children in branches.

## The Holiness of Wood

> *What did I know, what did I know*
> *of love's austere and lonely offices?*
> Robert Hayden

My father loved to return wrecks of old furniture
to the place where they once shone
with the holiness of wood.
He believed in things I could not see, things
which asked for hard work to get underneath
the veneer of damage, below even rawer places
from which there is no escape, below any hope.

I would see him for only moments in the furnace
and work room, sitting on cold basement concrete
next to a piece of furniture as if it
were his sick child, leaning there close,
in an old paint splashed t-shirt, dark trousers
with blotches bleached out from turpentine.
I never stopped to talk and my father did not look up.

He wanted to handle the sandpaper of truth
down in the basement and the soft cotton
polishing cloth of care in that place hope could not see
where he could do something, could return
something to life—and then carry up
from the underworld of our home
what he had made beautiful.

## There Is an Origin

For each true poem born there is an origin:
Blessed ignorance of words that turn
To splendid fire, as stars in space will yearn
To find on earth their up-stretched twin.

## Home Equity

God's hands over my head—
that's what a roof means!
But when I wake up in Spring light,
The only thing of worth is an open door.

## Prayer for a Quiet Mind and an Open Heart

Teach me

to set aside all thoughts of this and that,
to remain centered in the heart,
remember God, and let the rest flow past

to make a still breath or holy song
such company as to fill the day and leave behind
the endless chatter, clatter in the heart

to be open to the slightest pulse
of Light felt there and, beginning now,
to see God in all and everywhere.

## For a Friend Whose Faith in Me Is Like a Steady Flame

*She*

*sees*

*the core*

*of my being*

*gold, blue, star*

*light, opening*

*space filled with*

*nothing of this*

*world,*

*only Love.*

## Blown Home

Not finally brought home to God
by those mortals who know
how it all is and organize that
around the edges of words
that make up the towns
and train schedules
of understanding's itinerary,
nor even by the lovely vibrations
that linger after special evening concerts
of happy angels on tour through form,

but rather brought home by the wind
coming from way out there, unknown and holy,
beyond the sea cliff of solitude,
the same wind that since the beginning of longing
has been embraced to the core
by those who have flung their hearts
past the promontory of certainty
out into the open sea: simply to hear
a voice that meets their own
real as a spray of water
full on the face,
faithful as the sun
that sets or rises someplace
on earth always,

always the horizon
where the One soul of us all
is waveless and deep,
speaking of Love
night and day.

## Lift Up the Banner

Lift up the banner of your heart boldly
and commit your very next step
to what you love most dearly.
Such a banner is for the greatness
of wildflowers kissing their way delicately
through glaciers, for the beauty
of the mountaintop from which your soul
undoubtedly has gazed.
The next step you take shall bring you home
if you but release your cares
and think instead that help has come,
as sure as the wind will fly the banner
that you have raised —
the quietness of a wind
in an unseen meadow that waves
the banner of who you are
with the whispered assurance that says
*I Am.* Or the great, great wind
that fills your ship's sails announcing
your arrival to a throng of blue sky,
angelic presence's hushed in appreciation
of your arrival to the new world of a new day,
the blessed shore rushing up to greet you.

## Poetry

She skates boldly onto
the page, tips one vulnerable foot
back and forth slowly, till finally
the edge of a toe
cuts a simple, sharp line
through the world's cold resistance
and with that plain courage,
a statement of intention begins;
and you can't turn back any longer
from the weight of feeling and letting go
into the flow that follows.
Poetry is a choice to feel it all,
not all at once but gradually to sink down
within ourselves, to give what fear
we hold behind our knees
to gravity and grace,
to discover what makes
our whole world turn;
the place our necessary weight
lifts to lightened joy.

I am content to follow to its source
Every event in action or in thought;
Measure the lot; forgive myself the lot!
When such as I cast out remorse
So great a sweetness flows into the breast
We must laugh and we must sing,
We are blest by everything,
Everything we look upon is blest.

>William Butler Yeats
>from *A Dialogue of Self and Soul*